To our own little Dinosaurs:

Jermaine, Darion, Eli

© Jesse Seade 2020

The moral rights of the author have been asserted

All inquiries should be made to the author - jesse@atepixels.com

Printed in Australia by Ingram Spark

Typography lafriotnf, kitsu

Illustrated by: Ines M. Paulus

Written by: Jesse Seade

ISBN:

978-0-6489143-0-3: Paperback

978-0-6489143-1-0: Ebook - Epub

978-0-6489143-2-7 Ebook - Kindle

First published in 2020 by atepixels publishing - atepixels.com

The last naughty Dinosaur

Written by: Jesse Seade

Illustrated by: Ines M. Paulus

One night, when the moon was large and bright, and sitting really low in the sky,

Toli sneaked quietly into the village and covered the moon with his blanket.

So, after Toli had covered the moon it was super dark in the forest, too dark for any of the animals to find their way home.

There was only one available lamp in the forest and all the animals wanted to use it.

Giraffe took the first turn.

She went home, took a quick shower, put on her pj then returned the lamp to the other animals waiting outside.

Antelope had his turn next,

he went home, had a short soapy shower, had dinner, then returned with the lamp.

It was then Elephant's turn to use the lamp while the rest of the animals waited patiently outside his house.

Elephant took f o r e v e r!!

First he had a swim.

Then he had a bubble bath,

then decided maybe a little bit of yoga would help him calm down.

After that he played his guitar,

he scratched his back then had dinner.

After dinner Elephant started to feel sleepy so he decided to return the lamp.

Lion was not impressed as he watched elephant reappear with the lamp.

"**What took so long!**" he roared.

As soon as lion was about to enter his den,

the light went out.

Early the next morning, Elephant had no idea trouble was brewing outside.

When he opened his door to the first morning light, all he saw was the angry faces of all the other animals.

"We slept out here in the dark last night because of you, Elephant!!"

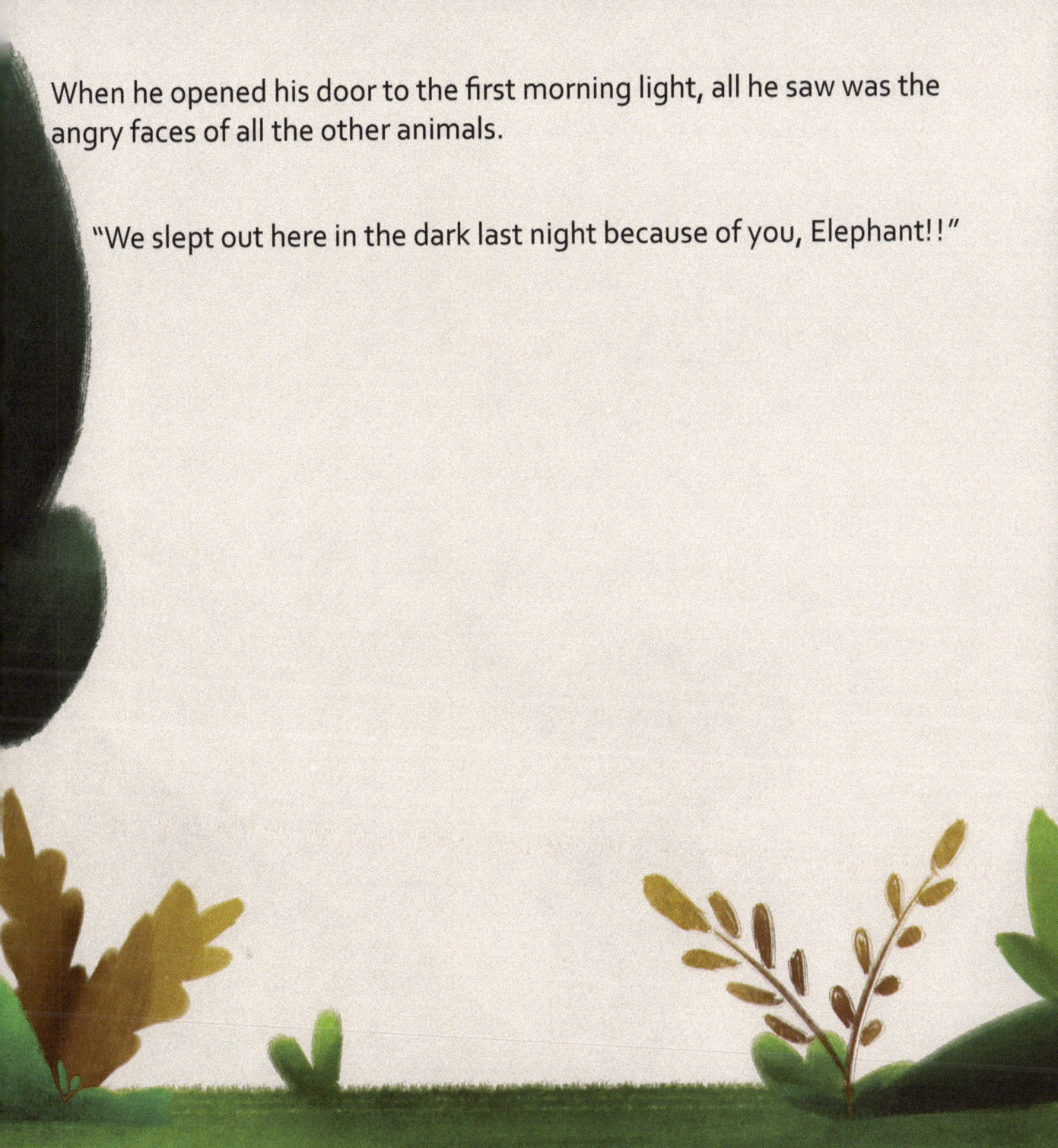

Elephant was a fixer, so he decided to fix the problem. He thought that by hiding Toli's blanket the moon will never be covered again.

So, with a beaming smile and confident stride, Elephant made his way up the steep! Steep! mountain where Toli lived alone.

On his way, he found Toli fast asleep on a patch of grass after a really long day being naughty.

Toli woke up with a start, both surprised and happy to see Elephant who was now puffed from the climb.

"Are you lost?" asked Toli. No one ever comes up here, he continued. " I am certainly not lost!!" came the reply. "I have come to ask you to come to dinner at my house."

"Really?!!" Asked Toli, who was now even more excited.

"I will race you down the mountain," said Toli,

but before he could finish the sentence,

Elephant was already tumbling down the mountain, so Toli tumbled right after him.

The tumbling was so loud it sounded like an earthquake,

but it wasn't....

Before long, they came crashing down at the bottom of the mountain, and it was so much fun.

Toli was so happy to have made a new friend he gave Elephant his blanket as a gift.

There was only one problem, there wasn't enough food to feed a Dinosaur,

because dinos eats lots! and lots! and lots of food.

The end.

The last naughty Dinosaur will be back with more naughty episodes

www.ingramcontent.com/pod-product-compliance
Lightning Source LLC
Chambersburg PA
CBHW061135010526
44107CB00068B/2946